S.S.F. Public Library
West Orange
840 West Orange Ave.
South San Francisco, CA 94080

South San Francisco Public Library

W9-AYF-688

NOV 1 4

My Favorite Dogs

GREAT DANE

Jinny Johnson

A+

Smart Apple Media

Published by Smart Apple Media,
an imprint of Black Rabbit Books
P.O. Box 3263, Mankato, Minnesota, 56002
www.blackrabbitbooks.com

U.S. publication copyright © 2015 Smart Apple Media.
International copyright reserved in all countries.
No part of this book may be reproduced in any form
without written permission from the publisher.

Edited by Mary-Jane Wilkins
Designed by Hel James

Cataloging-in-Publication Data is available from the Library of Congress

ISBN 978-1-62588-175-5

Photo acknowledgements
t = top, b = bottom
title page Jesus Souto; page 3 Vibe Images; 5 AnetaPics/
all Shutterstock; 7 Siri Stafford/Thinkstock; 8-9 Eric Isselee/
Shutterstock; 10-11 Lars Christensen/Thinkstock; 12t Guy
J. Sagi, b Erik Lam; 13t Maja H., b Birgit Sommer; 14 Maja H./
all Shutterstock; 15 Dale Spartas/Corbis; 16 Erik Lam/
Shutterstock; 17 Deanne Fitzmaurice/Corbis; 18 George Doyle/
Thinkstock; 19 Bernhard Richter; 20 Blaj Gabriel; 21 Roger costa
morera/all Shutterstock; 23 dmussman/Thinkstock
Cover Robynrg/Shutterstock

Printed in China

DAD0053
032014
9 8 7 6 5 4 3 2 1

Contents

I'm a Great Dane!

Yes, I am big, but I'm a gentle giant. Inside, I'm a sweetie.

I love my people and there's nothing I like more than curling up on the sofa to keep you company. There might not be room for you though!

What I Need

I do need exercise and
I like a walk every day.
Once I've had my walk
I'm a peaceful dog and
I'm happy to live in
an apartment.

I love being one of the
family and I want to join
in everything you do.

I do have a big appetite
and I need plenty of food!

The Great Dane

Short, glossy coat

Long, tapering tail

Color:
Brindle, fawn, blue, black, harlequin (white with black patches), mantle (black with white markings)

Height at shoulder:
Male at least 30 inches (76 cm); female at least 28 inches (71 cm)

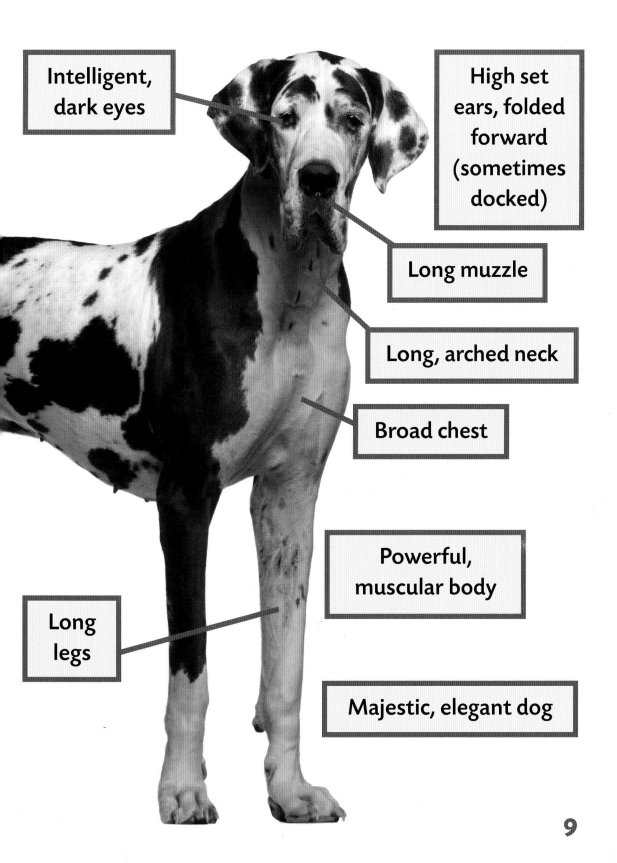

Intelligent, dark eyes

High set ears, folded forward (sometimes docked)

Long muzzle

Long, arched neck

Broad chest

Powerful, muscular body

Long legs

Majestic, elegant dog

9

All About Great Danes

The Great Dane was first bred in Germany, not Denmark.

These dogs were bred for speed and power in

The Great Dane has been the national dog of Germany since 1876.

boar hunts. Their ancestors were Irish wolfhounds, English mastiffs, and greyhounds.

Today Great Danes are bred as companion dogs.

Growing Up

A Great Dane pup is ready to leave his mom and brothers and sisters at eight weeks old.

There is nothing as cute as
a Great Dane pup
but he won't
stay small
for long!

Your little pup
will grow into
a **very big**
dog in no time.

Training Your Great Dane

Start training your Great Dane while he is still a pup and not too big. These dogs are heavy and strong and they must learn not to jump up. A Great Dane doesn't always know his own strength.

Teach your dog that you are in charge so he knows his place.

Great Danes drool and slobber a lot, so be prepared!

Danes are not bred as hunters today and should not be aggressive. Their loyalty and intelligence make them good guard dogs and they have a loud bark.

Supersize Dog

The Great Dane is one of the largest of all breeds and a full-grown male can weigh 200 pounds (90 kg). A dog of this size needs careful handling and lots of space.

Well-trained Great Danes are sweet natured and great with children. They're good with smaller dogs and other animals, too.

The world's
tallest ever dog
was a Great
Dane. George
was 7 feet
3 inches (2.2m)
standing on
his back legs.

Therapy Dog

The Great Dane's gentle, friendly nature makes it an ideal therapy dog. These dogs are taken into hospitals, schools, and other places to comfort people.

What could be nicer than
a hug from a Great Dane?

A therapy dog and his owner
do need special training and
the dog should be checked
by a vet every year.

Your Healthy Great Dane

The Dane's short coat is easy to look after, but giving a Great Dane a bath is not easy. Keep the coat in good shape with daily brushing and perhaps a dry shampoo from time to time.

Look after his nails, too, and have them clipped regularly.

Great Danes can suffer from hip and heart problems, so make sure you buy your pup from a good breeder. They can have tummy trouble, and should not do too much exercise just before or after meals.

Caring for Your Great Dane

You and your family must think very carefully before buying a Great Dane pup. He may live for ten years or more.

Every day your dog must have food, water, and exercise, as well as lots of love and care. He will need to go to the vet for checks and vaccinations. When you go out or away on vacation, you will have to plan for your dog to be looked after.

Useful Words

brindle
A coat color which is a mixture
of black with brown, tan, or gold.

breed
A particular type of dog.

vaccinations
Injections given by the vet to protect
your dog against certain illnesses.

Index